What Others Are Saying About The Author & This Book...

Tom is a grizzled veteran that has served our Nation across the globe for over 32 years and his powerful poetry and odes tell a story of his time in service. Warrior Dad encompasses a range of emotions that are heartfelt, loving and cathartic for folks that have experienced similar walks of life. The vivid illustrations help to convey powerful and inspirational messages from a Warrior Dad to his daughter.

—**Derek Baird** (the better-looking twin!)

"Warrior Dad Stories" is more than a book of odes—it's a bridge between the battlefield and family. As a Gold Star Spouse who watched my late husband miss those sacred moments, I know how powerful it is when fathers' voices are preserved in story. TJ's work honors that bond and reminds us that love and legacy can still be heard, even across the miles and years.

— **Bethanie MacDonald**, fellow Author and Gold Star Spouse

I have had the honor and privilege of serving alongside TJ for over three decades. He is a leader of uncommon character a friend who could always be counted on. Most of all, he is a devoted father in every sense. This book reflects the same experience, wisdom, and character that have defined who he truly is as a father, and man of principle.

—**Mike Alexander**, a fellow warrior

As a Warrior Mom, Wife, Sister, Daughter, Grandmother, I've watched Warriors Dads throughout my family quietly model what true adulthood is: discipline of yourself and your environment, patience, sacrifice and continually challenging yourself. As kids that's what we wanted to be. As adults, that's the kind of partner we sought. And continuing a family legacy, that's the career most of us chose.

—**Stephanie Hoehne,** First senior leader that hired TJ as a Nominative E9

Warrior Dad

Warrior Dad

TJ Baird

Warrior Dad
By: TJ Baird
Published by: Warrior Dad Stories

Publishing Consultant: Erin Marie at www.ErinMarieBooks.com

ISBN: 979-8-9933446-0-7
First Edition, 2026
Printed in the United States of America
10 9 8 7 6 5 4 3 2 1

To my daughter, the shining light in my life.
To my warrior wife, the one who makes this journey complete.
To my family, whose love anchors me no matter the distance.
To the warriors who stood beside me, carried the weight, and helped shape
the man and father behind these pages.
To those who listened, challenged, encouraged, and walked with me
through the creation of this book.
To every warrior and every child who keeps the light on.
To the families, the quiet strength we carry into every fight.
This book is for you.

Contents

Volume I: The Warrior's Oath

**"An oath is an unbroken promise.
It is lived in action, in sacrifice, in the heart."**

Ode to the Promise I Carried

One day, you stood there small and bright,
And I held your hand a moment tight.
No speech prepared, no perfect line,
Just love, and duty, intertwined.

I turned toward war, you stayed at home,
Yet your brave heart followed my own.
Across the sea, through dust and sand,
I carried you, not just my plan.

Not for applause, not to be seen,
But to come back to where you've been.
To keep my oath, to make it true,
To make it home, back home to you.

Every ode has a story—discover the journey behind the words at WarriorDadStories.com

Ode to the Guardian of Freedom

Oh, guardian bold, steadfast, and true,
Under the flag of red, white, and blue.

Through storm and sand, through fire and fight,
You stand unyielding, holding light.
Steel birds take flight in dawn's embrace,
Defending all with silent grace.

A sentinel with watchful eyes,
Protecting dreams beneath the skies.
No step unmeasured, none in vain,
Your oath endures through loss and pain.

And though the journey may be long,
Your heart beats strong in duty's song.

Every ode has a story—discover the journey behind the words at WarriorDadStories.com

Every ode has a story—discover the journey behind the words at WarriorDadStories.com

Ode to Hope Beyond Measure

The darkest night, the bitter cold,
Yet hope still shines in hearts so bold.

Through every trial, through every war,
The dream endures forevermore.

Not fear nor hate, not loss nor strife,
Can steal the pulse of freedom's life.

As long as voices dare to sing,
Hope will rise on eagle's wing.

Every ode has a story—discover the journey behind the words at WarriorDadStories.com

Every ode has a story—discover the journey behind the words at WarriorDadStories.com

Ode to the Road of Duty

The path is long, the miles stretch wide,
Yet love remains, our faithful guide.

Through distant lands, through skies unknown,
A beacon calls, our hearts come home.

For every step, for every year,
The dream of home is ever near.

Through war and storm, through night and day,
The road of duty finds its way.

Every ode has a story—discover the journey behind the words at WarriorDadStories.com

Ode to Those Beside Me

Shoulder to shoulder, hearts beat true,
Through fire, dust, and skies so blue.

We forge ahead, we stand as one,
A bond unbroken, battle-won.

No fear remains, no foe too tall,
For hand in hand, we never fall.

United strong, through thick and thin,
Together always, we shall win.

Every ode has a story—discover the journey behind the words at WarriorDadStories.com

Every ode has a story—discover the journey behind the words at WarriorDadStories.com

Ode to Triumph in the Face of Adversity

The road was rough, the sky turned black,
Yet still we marched and carried back.

Through dust and flame, through wounds and loss,
We bore the weight, we paid the cost.

Not broken down, not lost in pain,
We rise, we fight, we stand again.

For every trial, for all the scars,
We shine like steel, we reach the stars.

Every ode has a story—discover the journey behind the words at WarriorDadStories.com

Ode to the Forgotten Heroes

Their names are whispered in the breeze,
Their stories carried by the seas.
No parades, no golden prize,
Yet they still shine in watchful eyes.

For those who gave, for those who bled,
Who stood in ranks but went unsaid.
No song nor speech can match their grace,
But in our hearts, they hold their place.

Every ode has a story—discover the journey behind the words at WarriorDadStories.com

Ode to the Twilight Before Battle

The night leans in like an old friend,
its silence draped across our shoulders.

Under moonlight, I sit with purpose,
Tomorrow gathering in my chest.
Step by step I review the plan,
not rushed, just the rhythm of war.

The wind whispers through mountains and valleys,
like breath through a lullaby.
The moon is low.
A peace upon the land.

In that quiet moment, I think of her.
If morning brings fire, let this be the last calm I carry,
her face glowing in memory under a sliver of peace.

Every ode has a story—discover the journey behind the words at WarriorDadStories.com

Ode to Moonlight Over Patrol

We move in shadow,
boots over stone,
weight over silence.

The moon is a ball of silver
cutting across the ridge.

We walk like ghosts,
present, but unseen,
burdened by purpose,
held upright by habit.

I count every step,
not for the mission,
but for how many remain,
before I see her again.

Every ode has a story—discover the journey behind the words at WarriorDadStories.com

Volume II:
The Warrior's Gear, The Father's Heart

**"The gear bears the scars of battle.
The heart bears the reason we survive it."**

Ode to the Edge and the Barrel

In the hush before the breach,
my tools lie still; silent, sharp, and sure.
The blade, honed by years of quiet practice,
forges peace more than battle.

Beside it, the rifle hums in waiting,
a sentinel of thunder, loyal in its silence.
Both bear the weight of intent,
steel siblings under the same oath.

I place them side by side,
not as weapons,
but as symbols,
of duty, of readiness,
of the promise I made her:
to come back whole.

Every ode has a story—discover the journey behind the words at WarriorDadStories.com

Ode to the Ritual of Readiness

Every item has a home,
a reason, a role.
Gloves, mags, blades,
laid out like sacred relics.

My hands move with memory,
not rush.
This is not chaos,
this is deliberate purpose.

Readiness is an art form,
honed through repetition,
sharpened by need.

She once lined up her pencils beside me,
color by color,
order before joy.

Now I line up the tools of war,
and think of her with every placement.
Let the hunt begin.
But let love lead me back.

Every ode has a story—discover the journey behind the words at WarriorDadStories.com

Ode to a Warrior's Hands

These hands have held the line,
gripped steel in frost and purpose.

They've stitched torn packs,
pressed bandages to wounds,
and steadied trembling friends.

Beneath the worn leather,
callouses tell stories,
of endless drills, of sudden fire,
of writing her name
in the dust on my ruck.

I flex my fingers, feel the cold,
not from fear,
but from the absence of her touch.

Still, I keep them ready,
for every mission, every lifeline,
every hope I carry in her name.

Every ode has a story—discover the journey behind the words at WarriorDadStories.com

Ode to Muscle Memory

The sling bites across my chest,
a familiar pressure,
a father's quiet reassurance,
the echo of my hand in hers,
though we walk different ground.

The rifle rises without command,
because the body remembers
what the heart cannot forget.
Every mission, every breath,
etched into sinew,
stored in scars.

I trained for war.
But her voice, quieting my mind,
is what steadies my aim.

She reminds me
that this fight is not just duty,
it is devotion,
wrapped in her light,
moving forward.

Every ode has a story—discover the journey behind the words at WarriorDadStories.com

Every ode has a story—discover the journey behind the words at WarriorDadStories.com

Ode to the One Who Shook Me Awake

You found me above the world,
dead to it all;
five nights spent in shadows,
burning daylight and soul.

Raids behind us, rest ahead,
I collapsed into dreams,
not knowing Death
was creeping through the seams.

It started with thunder,
but I didn't wake.

Two hours of steel
rained down in waves,
and I...
I slept through hell
in shorts and sweat,
on a cot already claimed.

Then you came;
not quiet, not calm,
but alive and urgent,
a warrior's alarm.
You shook me to life
with the roar of a brother,
"WE ARE UNDER ATTACK"
just as the fire found cover.

Every ode has a story—discover the journey behind the words at WarriorDadStories.com

The blast chased your voice,
the world bent and screamed.

I ran blind in the night,
heart pounding, half-dreamed;
shorts, armor, my rifle,
no time for boots.

Just grit and survival
and your unshakable truth.
Three hours in the bunker,
we waited and swore
at the sky and its fire,
at the math of this war.

Every ode has a story—discover the journey behind the words at WarriorDadStories.com

And when I returned
to the ghost of my bed,
I saw the shrapnel
where I should've bled.

You gave me this time,
this borrowed breath,
this daughter's hug,
this defiance of death.
Because you didn't hesitate,
because you ran
into fire,
for me.

So, I live with the weight
of the life you preserved,
of the breath you gave back
without asking a word.

You didn't wait for glory,
or stand around for praise.

Heroes don't talk;
they move,
into fire,
into danger.
You'll never call it heroism.
But my daughter knows.

Every ode has a story—discover the journey behind the words at WarriorDadStories.com

Every ode has a story—discover the journey behind the words at WarriorDadStories.com

Ode to the Voice in the Storm

Crackling through the dust,
the radio stirs,
a ghost of order in chaos.

Commands ride the wind,
sharp as the sand stinging my face,
urgent as the heartbeat
racing beneath this plate.

But in the hush after the static,
I sometimes hear her voice,
or maybe I just wish I did.

Her quiet whispers,
now replaced by focused-need.
Her laugh, a subdued memory,
behind my war-born silence.

Still, I respond,
because I must.
Because in answering,
I carve a path back to her.

Every ode has a story—discover the journey behind the words at WarriorDadStories.com

Ode to the Final Check

The ruck leans into my spine,
its weight a second skin,
familiar, unforgiving.

Each strap cinched.
Each bolt, silent and smooth.

Optics clean, focused, ready.
not a smudge missed.

I kneel once more, to pray,
and to prepare.

My breath slows,
and in that stillness,
I picture her face,
the smile that steadies me
more than any battle drill.

When I rise,
the mission begins,
but so does the promise
to return.

Every ode has a story—discover the journey behind the words at WarriorDadStories.com

Ode to the Quiet Gaze

The world narrows to a sliver,
a breath, a flicker,
breath held before the mission.

My eyes; focused.
They've learned the patience
of a hunter who sees more
than targets.

Through dust and haze,
I watch.

Not with anger,
but with clarity.

There is danger ahead,
but I don't move toward it alone.

I carry her smile like a compass.
Even in this stillness,
she is with me.
Her love guides me.

Every ode has a story—discover the journey behind the words at WarriorDadStories.com

Ode to the Weight He Bears

Pressed to my chest,
this armor groans with memory.

It's not the weight of Kevlar,
but the souls it swore to shield.

Scratched, worn,
scarred like the men who wear it,
each mar whispers of what was endured,
what was deflected,
and what was felt anyway.

Her photo rests just beneath the plate.
She cannot see the battles,
but I feel her heartbeat between my ribs,
as if reminding me,
"Be brave, Dad! Come back to me."

Every ode has a story—discover the journey behind the words at WarriorDadStories.com

43
Every ode has a story—discover the journey behind the words at WarriorDadStories.com

Ode to the One I Return For

Each round I load is a vow,
not for vengeance,
but for protection.

Seven magazines, full and firm,
whisper beneath my gloves:
"Stay sharp. Stay alive."
These are not just brass and lead.

They are boundaries between chaos and return.
Each holds the hope of silence restored,
each shaped by the echoes
of her laughter across a distant ocean.

I do not fear the dark.
I move within it,
because the light in her eyes
waits for me to find my way home.

Every ode has a story—discover the journey behind the words at WarriorDadStories.com

Ode to the Silence Before Fire

The world holds its breath.
So do we.

Snow rests untouched,
not out of peace,
but anticipation.

I see the ridge through glass,
the edge between what we are
and what we might lose.

Behind me, they wait.
Behind them, memories.

Ahead, just one decision,
one breath, one shot,
that could take me farther from her.

47

Ode to the Shadows on the Land

The valley holds its scars.
Burn marks.
Destroyed vehicles.
Charred walls and broken roots.

We passed through here months ago,
or maybe years.
But the land remembers.
Always.

Still, green pushes through.
Tiny petals blooming
between shell cracks.
I step with care now.

Not for fear,
but respect.
Even here, where we tore the silence apart,
the earth forgives what men do not.

Every ode has a story—discover the journey behind the words at WarriorDadStories.com

Ode to the River's Lament

The water never stops.
It moves around stone and violence alike.
Casings glint in the current; war's jewelry,
forgotten by the weapons that ejected them.

The tracks we left on both banks
fade with every rain.
The river asks no questions.
It simply carries what remains.

I wonder, when she walks beside a stream someday,
will she know that I once crossed water
just like this, with boots soaked,
and prayers quiet on my lips.

Every ode has a story—discover the journey behind the words at WarriorDadStories.com

Ode to the Fallen Footsteps

Snow does not forget.
It holds every step,
like a breath held too long.

We climbed with caution,
each footfall a conversation,
between man and mission.

Some went up the ridge.
Not all returned.
No words for the others.
Just space, where voices used to be.

And snow, filling in what we left behind,
trying, but never quite covering it all.

Every ode has a story—discover the journey behind the words at WarriorDadStories.com

Volume III: The Road Home

**"The land forgets our names.
Home remembers them."**

Ode to Snow-Capped Heights

These mountains don't remember our names.
They've watched armies rise and vanish,
like breath on the wind.

Ice carves veins in ancient stone,
etched by time, filled with memories of the past.
Below, we scratch out a presence,
tents, vehicles, smoke, the hum of war,
but none of it disturbs the range.

I stand in awe,
not of what I carry,
but of what refuses to move.

She is like this range,
unshaken by distance,
anchored in love.

Every ode has a story—discover the journey behind the words at WarriorDadStories.com

Ode to Distant Summits

I sit above the noise.
Below, war stirs in slow rhythm,
up here, time forgets its urgency.

My ruck is at rest beside me.
My eyes trace the edge of every ridge.
I do not speak.

The mountain does not answer.
But we understand each other.

I came with orders.
I stay for breath.

For a moment, I remember what it feels like
to not be watched, but to simply be.

And I think of her in quiet.

Every ode has a story—discover the journey behind the words at WarriorDadStories.com

Ode to the Silent Watch

Beneath the stars, the wind runs cold,
The desert speaks in whispers old.
I stand my post, I hold the line,
Yet hear your voice, so soft, so fine.

No lantern near, no guiding flare,
Just memory moving through the air.
Your laughter lives where shadows start,
A steady watch inside my heart.

I guard this ground, I face the night,
But you are still my truest light.

Every ode has a story—discover the journey behind the words at WarriorDadStories.com

Ode to the Quiet Trace

Our post is empty now.
Sandbags slouched.
Wind pulling loose tape like ribbon.

No struggle.
No fire.
Just silence.

We packed and moved without fanfare.
A warrior's departure is not marked by noise,
but by absence.

Our prints fade in the frost,
brittle, shallow, gone before the sun can rise.

Every ode has a story—discover the journey behind the words at WarriorDadStories.com

Ode to a Soldier's Prayer

I knelt, not to be seen,
not to be heard,
but because there was nowhere else
to place what I carried.

Light streamed from the heavens,
not for them, not for me.
But because some weight deserves a witness.

I left my helmet by my side,
not out of ritual, but release.
And in the silence, I asked nothing,
and hoped for peace.

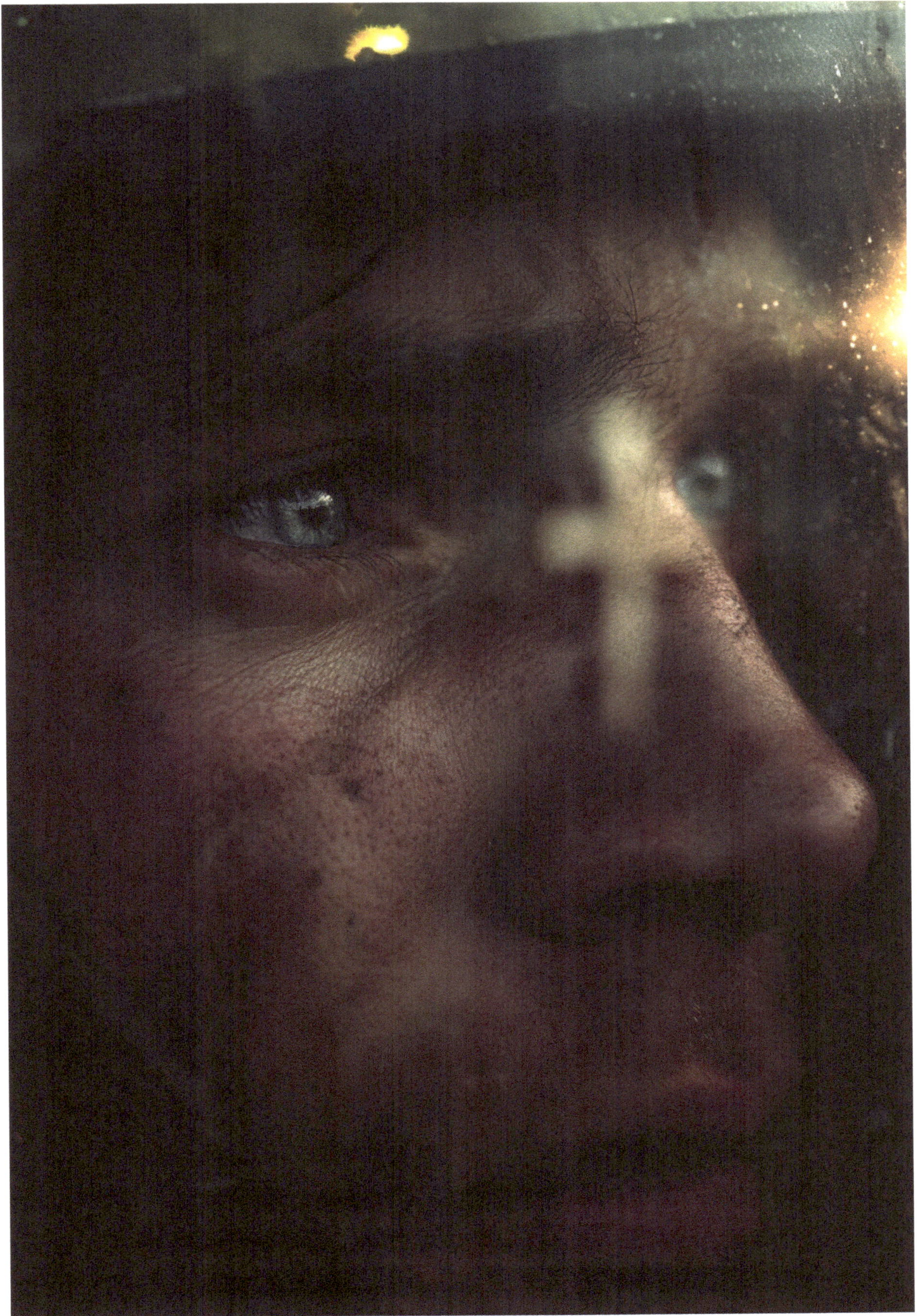

Every ode has a story—discover the journey behind the words at WarriorDadStories.com

Ode to My Guiding Star

Across the sea, beyond the sand,
I hear your voice, soft yet grand.
A whispered laugh, a lullaby,
A memory bright beneath this sky.

No matter where this duty calls,
Your love stands strong, it never falls.
You are the light that leads me true,
And every step, I walk for you.

Every ode has a story—discover the journey behind the words at WarriorDadStories.com

Ode to a Soldier's Last View

The sun dipped low,
casting fire on the ridgeline.

I watched it burn,
not with fear, but with thanks.

I have made it this far.
I have held the line.
I am coming home to her.

My breath stilled,
a pause, not an ending.

And I thought,
if this is the last thing I see,
let it be this peace.

Every ode has a story—discover the journey behind the words at WarriorDadStories.com

Ode to the Long Road Home

My path fades behind me,
snow claiming the weight I left.

The mountain does not wave goodbye.
It does not mourn.
It simply stands.

And I carry what I must.
I move forward,
not because combat is over,
but because love waits ahead.

The wind wipes clean,
what once marked our passage.

She cannot trace the path,
but I remember the way,
etched in her love for me.

Every ode has a story—discover the journey behind the words at WarriorDadStories.com

Ode to the Distance Between Us

A world away, I miss you so,
Each night I dream, I watch you grow.
The days are long, the miles wide,
Yet love endures, a faithful guide.

Your laughter lifts, your letters shine,
They build a bridge from yours to mine.
No space, no war, no time too vast,
For bonds like ours will always last.

Every ode has a story—discover the journey behind the words at WarriorDadStories.com

Ode to the Gift of Love

You sent your light, a gift of love,
A steady strength from far above.
In darkest hours, in cold and sand,
I felt your hope held in my hand.

Your light became my quiet shield,
A warmth the war could never steal.
It walked me through the longest nights,
It brought me back through distant fights.

And now I'm home, my duty done,
Your light guided me back to where I'd begun.
The gift was not what I could hold,
But love that kept my spirit bold.

Every ode has a story—discover the journey behind the words at WarriorDadStories.com

Ode to the Moment Time Stood Still

The road is long, the sky turns bright,
Homeward bound, my heart takes flight.

Your words were warmth in midnight's chill,
Now I am here, and time stands still.

And as I see your face so true,
Your shining eyes of the perfect you,

I kneel and hold you, safe at last,
No more goodbyes, just love so vast.

Every ode has a story—discover the journey behind the words at WarriorDadStories.com

Ode to a Daughter's Light

Through battle's call and distant land,
I march ahead with steady hand.
Yet in the dark where shadows grow,
Your love's the light that guides me home.

The echoes of the war drums fade,
Yet one soft voice will never wane.
A laughter bright, a lullaby,
The melody that fills my sky.

You sent your light to walk with me,
A guiding flame that set me free.
Through endless night and restless fight,
It held the line, it burned so bright.

And now I walk that road once more,
A journey past the battlefield's door.
But this time, daughter, have no fear,
I stand in your light, I'm home, I'm here.

For love endures where war must cease,
And duty bows to hands of peace.
No miles can part, nor time erase,
The light you give, my saving grace.

I will never forget what pulled me through,
The gift you gave, the love so true.
The path was lit, through dark and dread,
Because your love for me had led.

Every ode has a story—discover the journey behind the words at WarriorDadStories.com

Every ode has a story—discover the journey behind the words at WarriorDadStories.com

<u>**Image Descriptions**</u>

- 2021 Visit to Chincoteague with V-Star- A weekend bike ride around the island!
- 2018 Hunting with V-Star- First hunting trip with V-Star! She was an awesome spotter!
- 2003 Dave and I in Nuristan- Dave and I just entering one of the valleys in Nuristan. We conducted a multi-week operation searching for weapons caches and enemy combatants... very successful!
- 2017 Shooting with Cool Bear- A close-up of my target with Cool Bear as my "coach!" This was a fun day on the range; competition shooting against my young soldiers who challenged the "old guy."
- 2003 Patrolling on the border- This is a random tough guy photo while on patrol on the AF/Pak border.
- 2025 Road trip to visit V-Star- We braved the weather to take a walk around the lake at a national park near V-Star's university.

- 2004 Winter in the mountains- Yes, we eventually made it to the top of the ridgeline during a series of operations. Yes, it was damn cold!
- 2017 Cool Bear on the range- This is the bear my daughter gave me prior to my last deployment. As you can see, he is a pretty good shot.
- 2004 river in Nuristan- Back in Nuristan for another operation. We crossed this river several times. This river is the inspiration to The Ode to the River's Lament.
- 2002 MFF Jump Training- This was my first Military Freefall jump training event. I took this picture using a wind-up Kodak camera that we taped to my helmet.
- 2022 Fun photo with the coolest kid- A random fun photo while running errands.
- 2003 MSS PANO- composite panoramic photo from our position on the border. This was put together before cameras and software came standard with a panoramic function.

Every ode has a story—discover the journey behind the words at WarriorDadStories.com

A Note of Gratitude

This book exists because of the men and women around the world who choose, every day, to stand in service to something greater than themselves. Their sacrifices, often unseen and unrecognized, form the quiet foundation of the freedoms we live under and the lives we can build. To those who serve, past and present, your commitment, courage, and resilience continue to inspire far beyond the uniform.

Along the way, I lost many friends. Some were United States service members. Others were men and women who stood up to tyranny in their own countries, choosing courage over safety and hope over fear. I also honor those who made the ultimate sacrifice in service to this nation and to the cause of freedom. Their lives, their resolve, and their legacy are never forgotten.

This book is written with respect for the weight they carried and the cost they paid, and with enduring gratitude from a nation and a fellow warrior forever shaped by their service. You are remembered, you are honored, and your watch continues in ways we cannot yet fully see.

9 798993 344607